CO

ABOUT THE AUTHOR

Mrs Niti Kumar

Niti Kumar is an Indian Cultural Ambassador based in Chiba Prefecture, Japan, an author, certified Ayurveda massage therapist and an accomplished cook in Japan.

Niti moved to Japan from India in 1979 after marriage. As she was humbled by the support and love she received from her Japanese friends and community and wanted to give back to the country that had welcomed her and accepted her as their own, she started Indian cooking classes. She also started Ayurveda massage after her training in Bangalore and Goa, India. In addition, she is currently certified in baby massage, Abhiyanga, Ayur Yogic massage, Ayur Balancing Massage, Marma Point Massage, Maternity massage, Reflexology and Panchkarma. And aroma therapy course from Kannauj. Niti has been a practicing Ayurvedic massage therapist for more than a decade and has had great success with her clients/patients.

Her passion and dedication to bring Indian culture to Japan resulted in her receiving multiple awards and certificates. She has been featured on Japanese TV, magazines and newspaper. In 2011 she went on to publish her first massage book in three languages-English, Japanese and Hindi.

In 2017 Niti has conducted "Ayur Balancing Massage" certificate course in Japan. Niti is currently teaching Ayurvedic baby massage to Japanese parents in Japan.

PREVENTION IS BETTER THAN CURE

Since ancient times people have healed the human body through different types of massages; whether it was through vigorous pushing, gentle rubbing or rhythmic tapping, massages have been a big part of healing through various civilizations. Hippocrates, known as the Greek God of Medicine, said that the effect of massage is to make the tight joints soft and soft joints strong. Socrates, Plato, Heraclitus have each written about the effect of massage in ancient Greece. Massages were popular in ancient Egypt as well. Pictorial evidences of massages have been found on grave stones in Egypt.

There are varied opinions of the origin and etymology of the word massage which has been passed on from generation to generation through different parts of the world. For example, massage in Arabic, called Mashu, means to push gently; in Greek, called Masen, means to knead; in French, Mashel means to shampoo, and in old Chinese document massage is written as the act of healing one's body.

In recent times, despite the advent of electrical massage equipment people are strongly turning to original hand massages because the effect of good hand massage has much more impact on human body. The Indian science of Ayurveda, which means to live healthy life, believes that massages help blood circulation that lead to healthy body and healthy mind. According to Ayurveda, there are different types of massages appropriate for different ages such as infant massage, youth massage, adult massage, pregnant women massage, nursing mothers' massage, elderly person massage, as well as massages for specific conditions. Ayurveda believes body should be maintained through massages even before one gets sick – prevention is better than cure-and to live life energetically it is important to get regular massages.

Massages use various kinds of oils to help aid massage. The selection of oils varies based on each individual, their physical condition at that time, and the climate. I usually use pure sesame oil which is known for its excellent nourishment and antioxidant properties. Depending on the person, I sometimes mix 1-2 drops of aroma oil in the sesame oil. However, I would caution against mixing aroma oil unless one is very familiar with aroma oil because if the proportion and properties of aroma oil are not well known it may have harmful side effects.

BABY MASSAGE

For an infant baby, who has grown up in the mother's womb getting its nourishment through the umbilical cord, gets a shock when it comes out of the amniotic fluid to live by itself in the environment. Baby's life outside the womb begins with the change of the pulmonary respiration. The massage can soften big changes in the environment and the shock at this time. Moreover, massage helps release the amniotic fluid that enters the infant's body during birth.

If a mother massages her infant by hand for 7 minutes a day, not only does she bond with the baby but the circulation generated through the massage helps in removing the radicals and improving the function of the body, internal organs and spirit of the child (skeletal system, muscle system, nervous system, lymphoid system, circulatory system, sensory system, respiratory system, digestive system, excretion system, sexual organs system, and as well as emotional etc.). Massages help make a great foundation for child's healthy mind and body.

LEG MASSAGES

Lay the baby down on his back and look in his eyes.

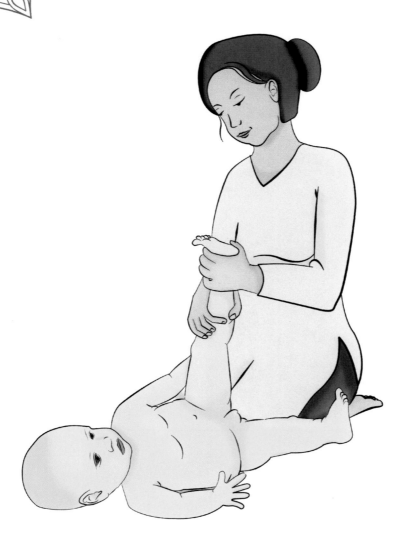

01

Hold the baby's ankle with your right hand and with the palm of your left hand, gently massage in upward strokes from ankle towards the thigh 4-5 times without any oil. Now hold the ankle in the left hand and with your right hand gently massage in upward strokes 4-5 times.

LEG MASSAGES

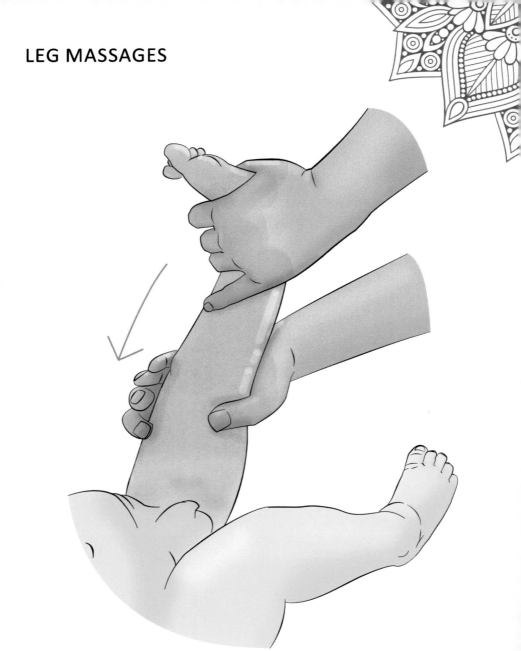

02

Put oil on your hands and massage in the same way as mentioned above applying a little more pressure/strength than before.

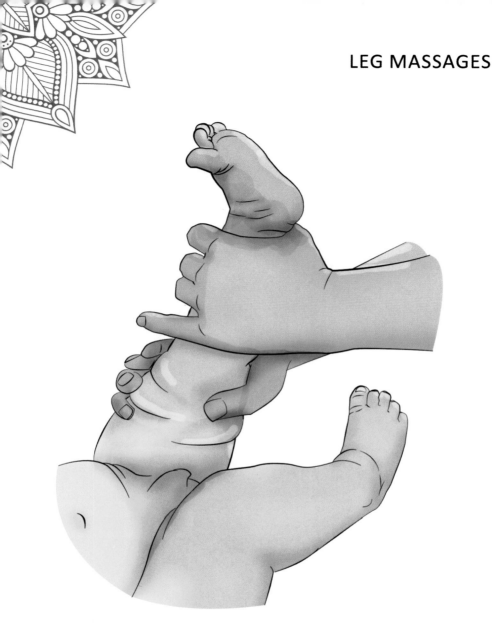

03

Hold the baby's ankle with your left hand and with you right hand twist leg muscles anticlockwise at the 3 places from the ankle to thigh.

- Change your hand and twist back the muscles

- Finally massage the leg 2-3 times in upward moving strokes from ankle to thigh, applying a little more pressure/strength to settle the muscles down

● Repeat step 3, applying a little more pressure while twisting the baby's leg muscle.

LEG MASSAGES

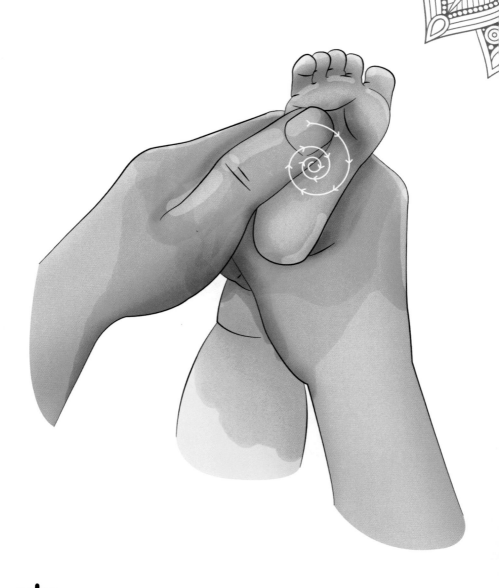

04

Put oil on your thumbs and draw spiral on the baby's sole. (Make sure that you do not lift your thumb from the sole as you are drawing the spiral).Retrace the your thumb back to the starting point of the spiral.

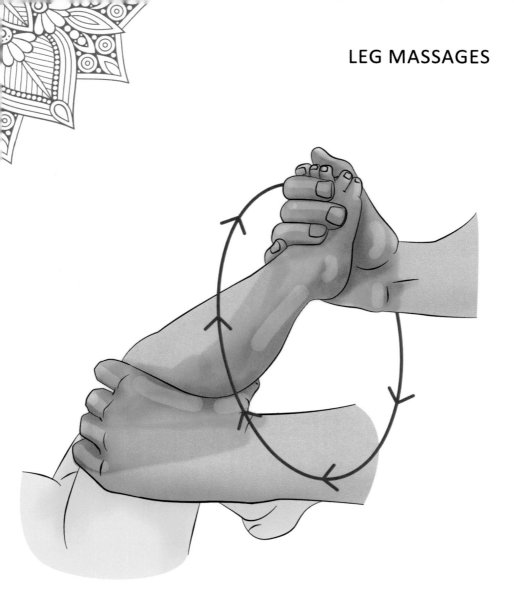

05

Hold the baby's knee with your left hand and hold the baby's toe with your right hand, now turn the baby's ankle towards right 3~5 times. (Repeat by turning the ankle left, up, and down in the same way.)

LEG MASSAGES

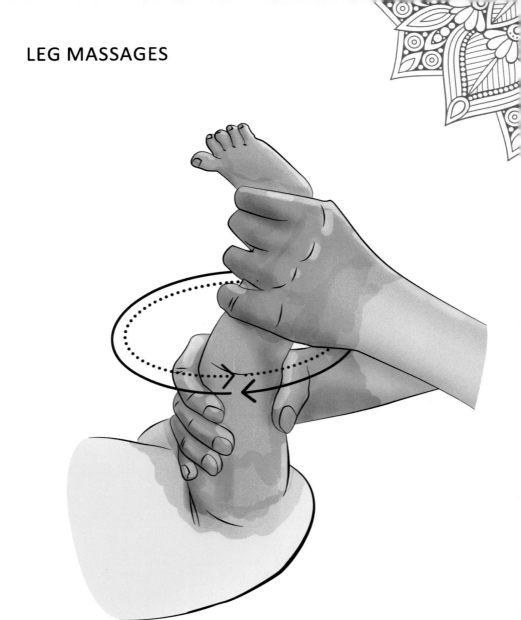

06

Hold the baby's thigh a little above the knee wit your left hand, and the baby's toe with your right hand and turn in the same way as 6.

● Repeat same process of A 1-7 with the other leg

STOMACH MASSAGES

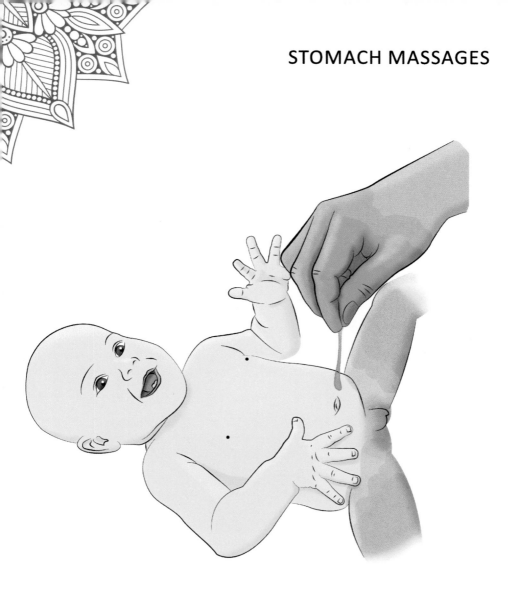

01 Pour a little oil in the baby's navel, and put your fingertips on the navel.

STOMACH MASSAGES

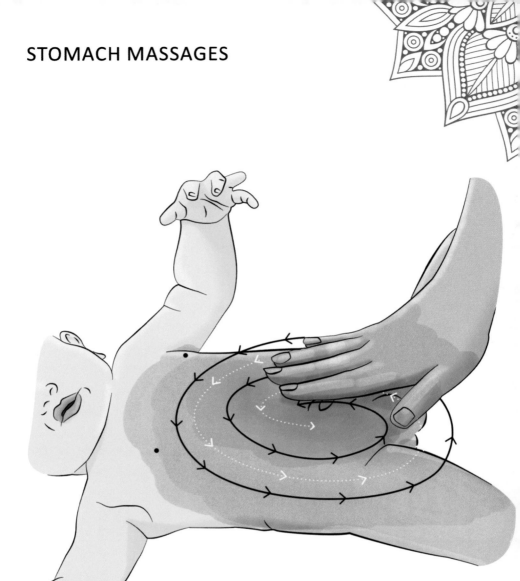

02

Draw a big spiral clockwise around the navel. Without lifting your fingers from the abdomen trace back the spiral motions back to the navel. Press the navel once softly.

● In case of diarrhea - make the spiral motions anticlockwise. However during constipation or regular bowel movement continue with clockwise motions

STOMACH MASSAGES

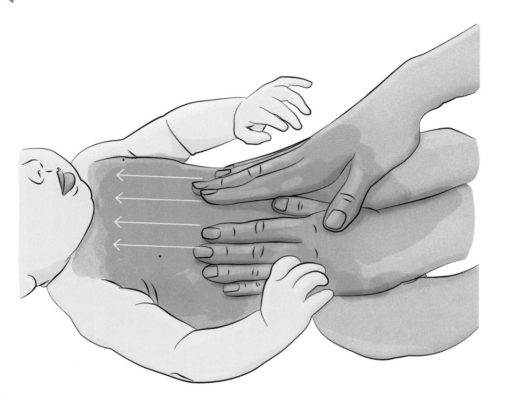

03

Put oil on your hands and massage in upwards strokes from under the navel to the shoulders.

- Massage 2-3 times to spread oil all over the abdomen

STOMACH MASSAGES

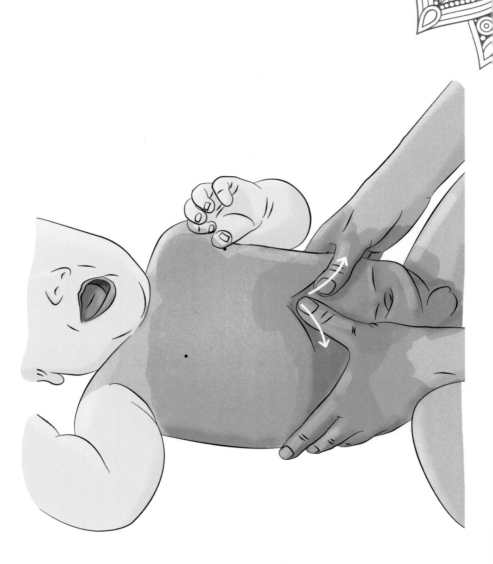

04

Put your thumbs under the bottom ribs. Stroke along the bones from the center towards the waist.

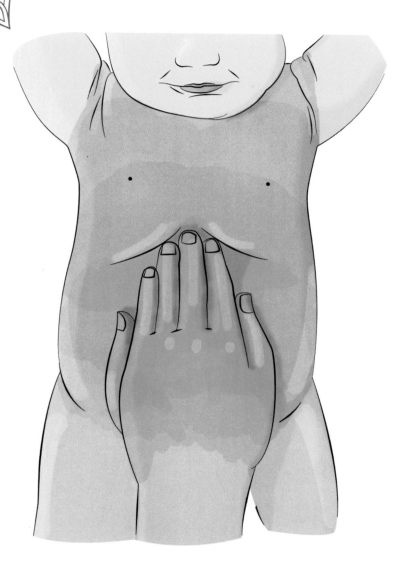

05

Put your fingertips on center of the rib and add little pressure for three seconds.

STOMACH MASSAGES

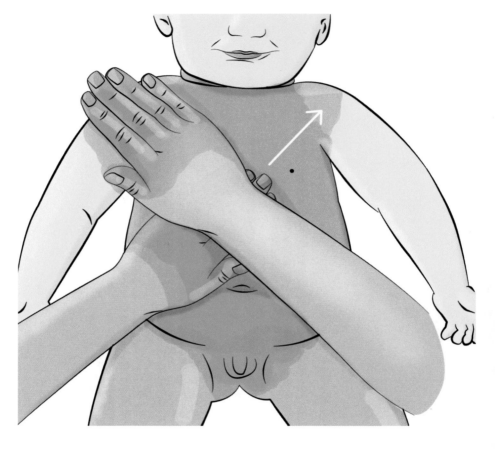

06

Keep your right palm on the right side of the rib and massage towards the left shoulder with diagonal strokes and simultaneously with the left hand massage from left rib towards the baby's right shoulder.

● Do this 3-4 times.

STOMACH MASSAGES

07 Put both your thumbs on the center of the clavicle. Massage the baby with strokes moving towards the shoulders along the clavicle.

HAND MASSAGES

01 Put oil on your hands. Hold the baby's wrist and massage them in upward stroke from the wrist to the shoulder a few times.

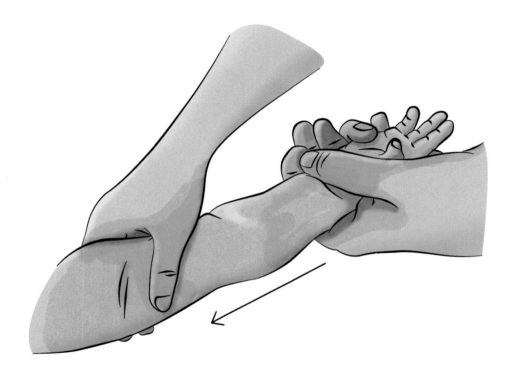

02

Hold the baby's wrist with your left hand and the arm with your right hand.

● massage in the same way as mentioned above applying a little more pressure/strength than before.

HAND MASSAGES

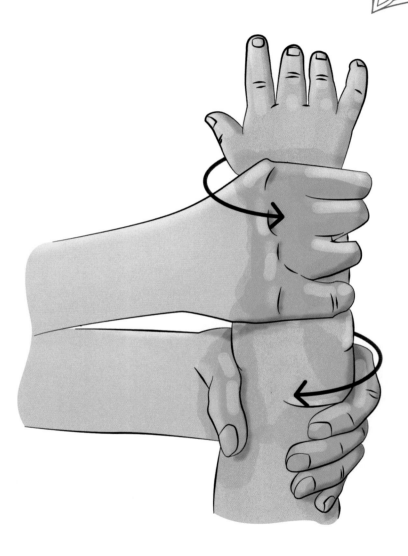

03

Hold baby`s hand as shown in sketch, then twist counterclockwise, change hand and twist clockwise.

- Stroke in the same way as (01) applying a little more pressure/strength to settle the muscles down. Change the hand and do the same.

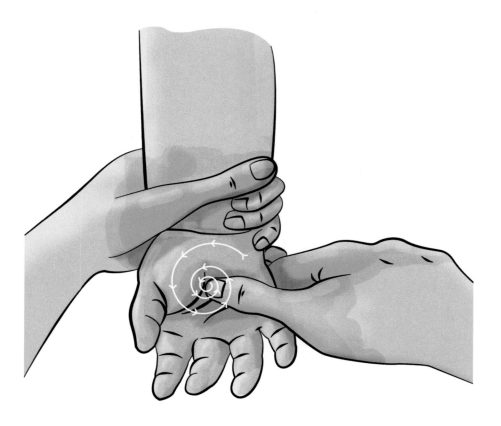

04 Put oil on your thumb. Draw spirals from the center to the outside on the baby's palm. Without lifting your fingers from the palm, retrace the motion back to the center drawing spirals.

HAND MASSAGES

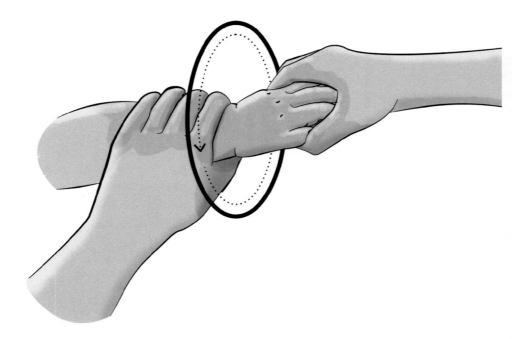

❀
05
❀

Hold your baby's hand just above the wrist with one hand and with the other hand move the baby's wrist right and left 3-5 times in a circular motion.

HAND MASSAGES

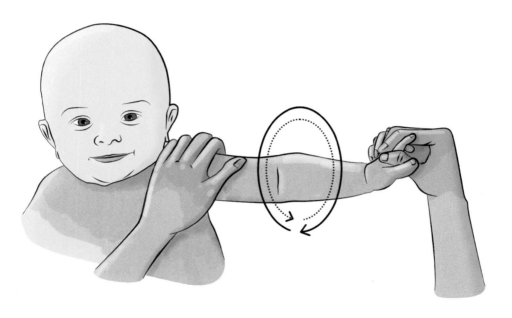

06

Hold the baby's shoulder with one hand and with the other hand hold the baby's palm then rotate the baby's shoulder in circular motion.

FACE MASSAGES

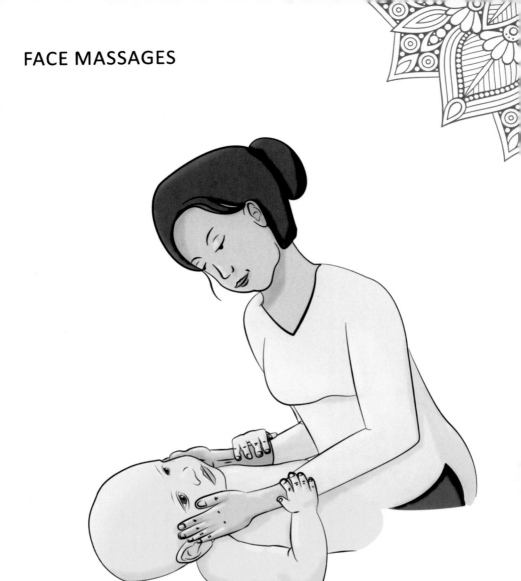

01

Wrap the baby's face with your hands, without using oil in your hand. Massage baby's face with your palms with strokes.

- Moving from the chin to the forehead 3-5 times.

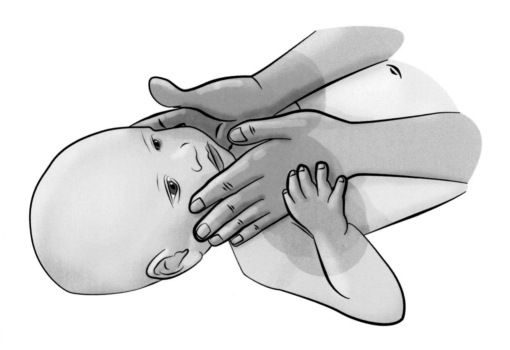

02

Put oil on your hands. Repeat the same massage as above.

FACE MASSAGES

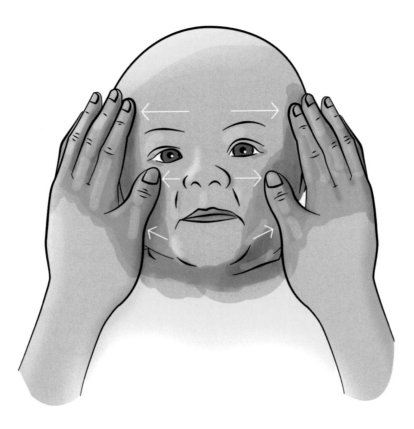

03 Put your palms on either side of the chin and massage horizontally by sliding your thumb on eithersides simultaneously. Start from center of the chin sliding your thumb towards the outside, repeat same with lips, then nose, then eyes and finally the forehead.

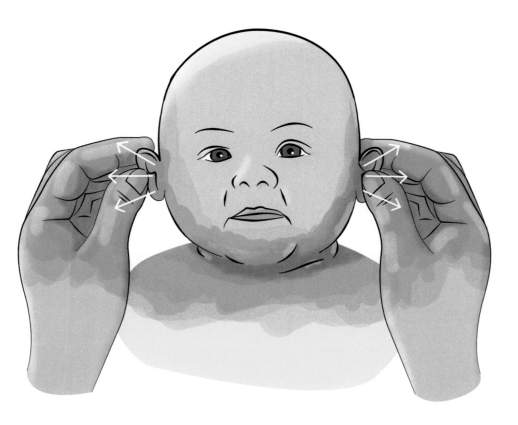

04 Put oil on your finger and hold the baby's ears and gently pull them out a few times.

FACE MASSAGES

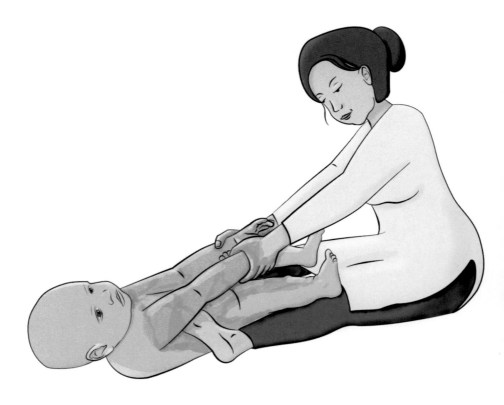

05

As you sit down, put your feet under your baby`s armpits. Hold on to baby`s hands gently pulling the baby towards yourself raising his shoulders above the ground. Now remove your feet but keep holding the baby`s hands.

- Raise him up counting 1-2-3

🔴 Do this from 1 year old baby.

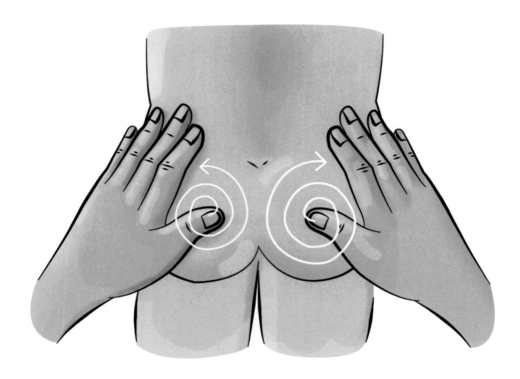

01

Put oil on your hands. Draw circular spirals on both of the baby's buttocks with your thumbs.

HIP MASSAGES

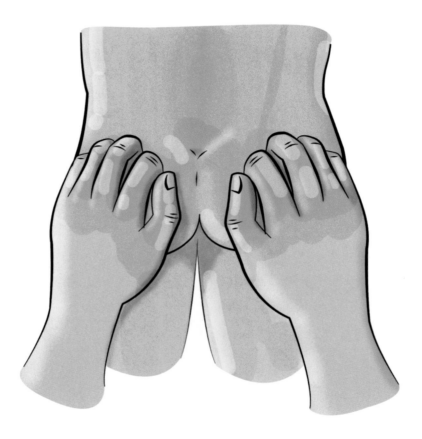

02

Grasp the baby's hips with both your hands at the same time.

● Do this 2-3 times.

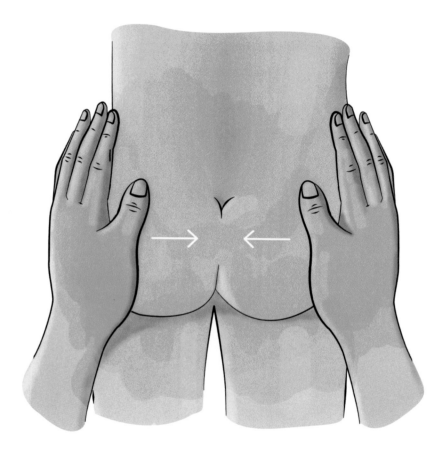

03

Placing them on either side of the baby's buttocks massage towards the middle of the buttocks ending with a clapping sound.

● Do this 2-3 times.

BACK MASSAGES

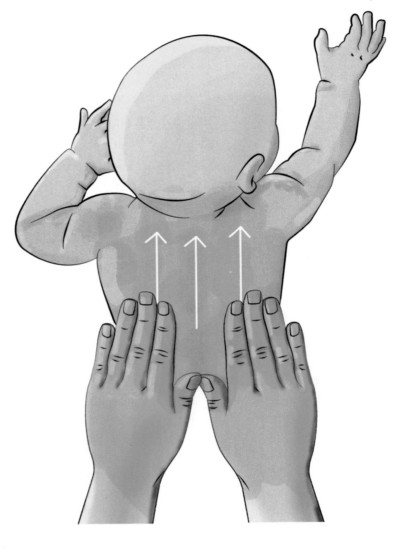

01 Put oil on your hands. Massage in upward strokes from the waist to the shoulders with your both hands a few times so that oil is spread all over the back.

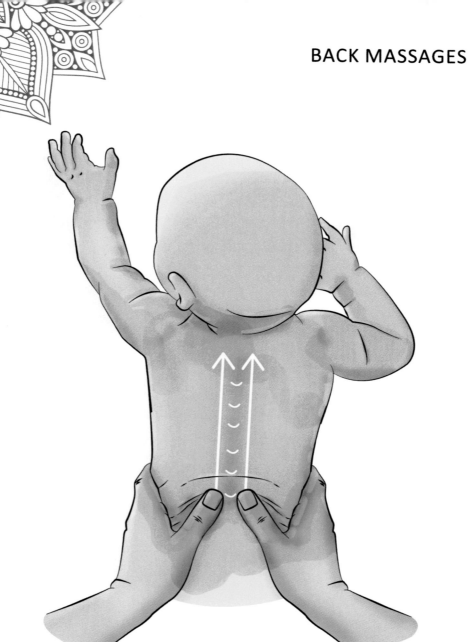

02 Put your thumbs on either side of the backbone and massage with your thumb in upward moving strokes from the waist to the shoulder along the backbone.

BACK MASSAGES

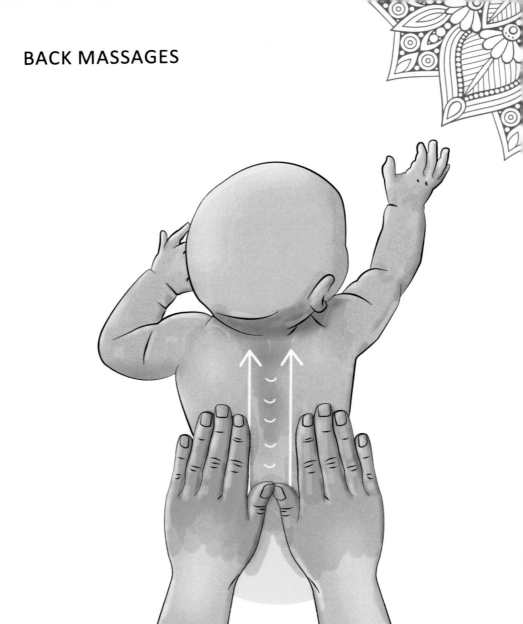

03

With your both the hands massage the baby on the backbone from the waist to the shoulders in upward moving strokes to settle the muscle down.

NECK MASSAGES

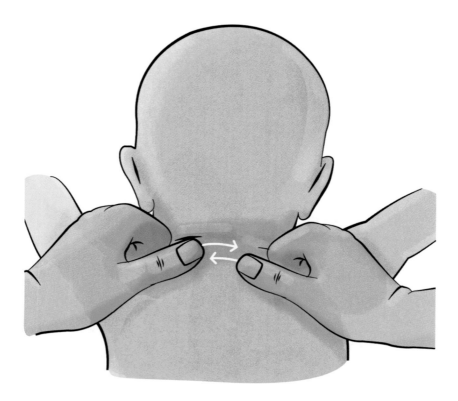

01 Put oil on your thumbs. Place both the thumbs between the bones of the neck one over the other and slide them horizontally toward the cervical vertebrae on either sides simultaneously.

NECK MASSAGES

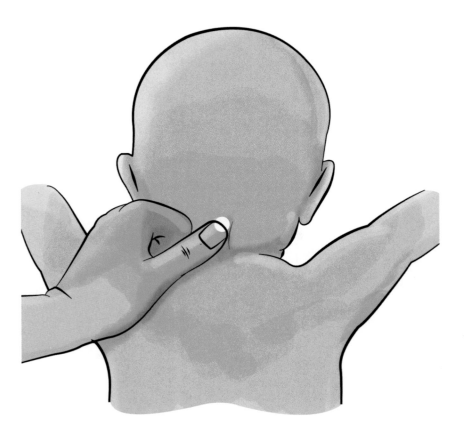

02

Press your thumb on the center of the back of the skull for 3-5 seconds.

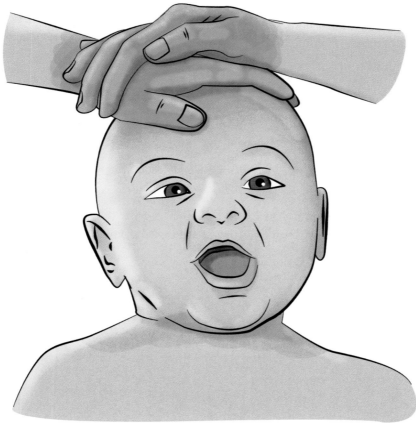

01 Put oil on the top of the baby's head and tap gently with your palms 5-7 times.

ATTENTION

- Enjoy massage with your baby. Talking to him and staring into each other's eyes

- You may apply more or less pressure in your strokes depending on the baby's condition

- Don't worry if the child is crying because CRYING makes the lungs strong

- Do the massage with with strokes moving towards the heart as the blood flows towards the heart

- Do Not give massage after baby's bath

- Give a massage as you press marma points(acupressure points)

- Beside sesame oil you can use baby oil, olive oil, raw mustard oil, raw salad oil. Or whatever oil you have but it should be raw

● This book is written mostly based on what I have learned in India referencing to the litrature and HP.

TESTIMONIALS

My 5 months old son (Shousei) had severe eczema for which the dermatologist prescribed a steroid ointment. As I didn't want to use steroids, I consulted my friend who introduced me to Mrs. Kumar and her Ayurveda baby massage class.

My husband was against this massage but now that my son is stronger and healthier without medication he is very supportive of Ayurveda baby massage and together with me thankful to Mrs. Kumar from the bottom of our hearts.

- Ryoko (Mother)

A friend recommended me to see Niti Kumar for ayurvedic massage therapy for general well-being of the child when my 8 month old baby girl (Ema) developed high fever for the first time after birth and I was very worried.

Just after one session of massage by Mrs. Kumar my baby was fever free, which surprised me and made me very curious to learn this art of naturally taking care of my child.

Once I started the Ayurveda Baby massage therapy as a routine I was very pleased to see the gradual changes in my child. And now after a year and a half of massage therapy I have a very happy and healthy kid who is not shy to meet new people and loves eating all kinds of food.

- Ai Akiyama (Mother)

TESTIMONIALS

My son (Aoba) was about 18 months old but to me seemed to be weak for his age. I consulted Mrs. Niti Kumar who suggested I massage him with different aromatic oils in each stage of her Ayurveda Baby massage classes.

I worried when he cried a lot or at times had eczema which Mrs. Niti said were signs of detoxing but I could see my baby became stronger and stable physically and mentally and continued the massaging.

I cannot explain it but I do believe that he is now growing up as a healthy and positive boy because of the Ayurveda Baby massage.

- Mihoko Sakamoto (Mother)

My daughter (Kokomi) had infantile eczema for which in accordance to instructions by the doctor, I stopped giving her egg, milk, bread etc and started applying a steroid ointment.

I consulted Mrs. Niti who was my Pranayam instructor and was advised to join her Ayurveda Baby massage lesson. Now my daughter has stronger skin than before and almost no eczema even though I have started giving her egg, milk and bread twice or thrice in a week. I`m really thankful to Mrs Niti and her Ayurveda Baby massage.

- Matsui Yukari (Mother)

TESTIMONIALS

My second daughter, Madoka couldn't hold her head up until she was 10 months old and as she was diagnosed with Hypotonia (floppy baby) we started her training at a rehabilitation center but this unfortunately didn't produce desired results.

I met Mrs. Kumar when my daughter was 2 years old and started taking her Ayurveda Baby massage classes. Frankly speaking, I didn't believe the massage could change my daughter but I thought it is always better to do something than nothing.

After I started the class I realized that I myself was being healed through the physical contact with my daughter. Amazingly, Madoka also looked very relaxed. Seeing this even my 5 years first daughter also asked me to massage her.

After six months of this massage, Madoka had febrile convulsion and had to be hospitalized for a week. Mrs. Kumar said it was the result of changes in her body and therefore a good change, though it was a terrible experience for me.

And really it happened! After this incident, Madoka started crawling and standing. I could feel her develop physically and intellectually. She thereafter started walking with support and beyond our expectation got admission in a kindergarten as we had always thought she would never go to a normal school because of her lack of intellectual development. Now she is enjoying school and can get along with her friends. You will not believe it but she can walk by herself. She can do more things than I could ever imagine.

I had taken her to all places, wherever I heard she will become normal, for treatment. Training at the rehabilitation center was very good but this Ayurveda Baby massage was like a magic to her and me.

- Shinobu Inoue (Mother)

My special Thanks to

Lt. Shri Brij Behari Sahai (Babuji) And

Lt. Smt. Gomti Devi (Amma)

Akhilesh Kumar (My husband)

For Helping me

Anit, Shivika, Ashvik

For giving me inspirations

Atin, Ratna And Aarit

For encouragement

Mrs Seema Kumar (Niece)

English Translation

Made in the USA
Las Vegas, NV
14 January 2025